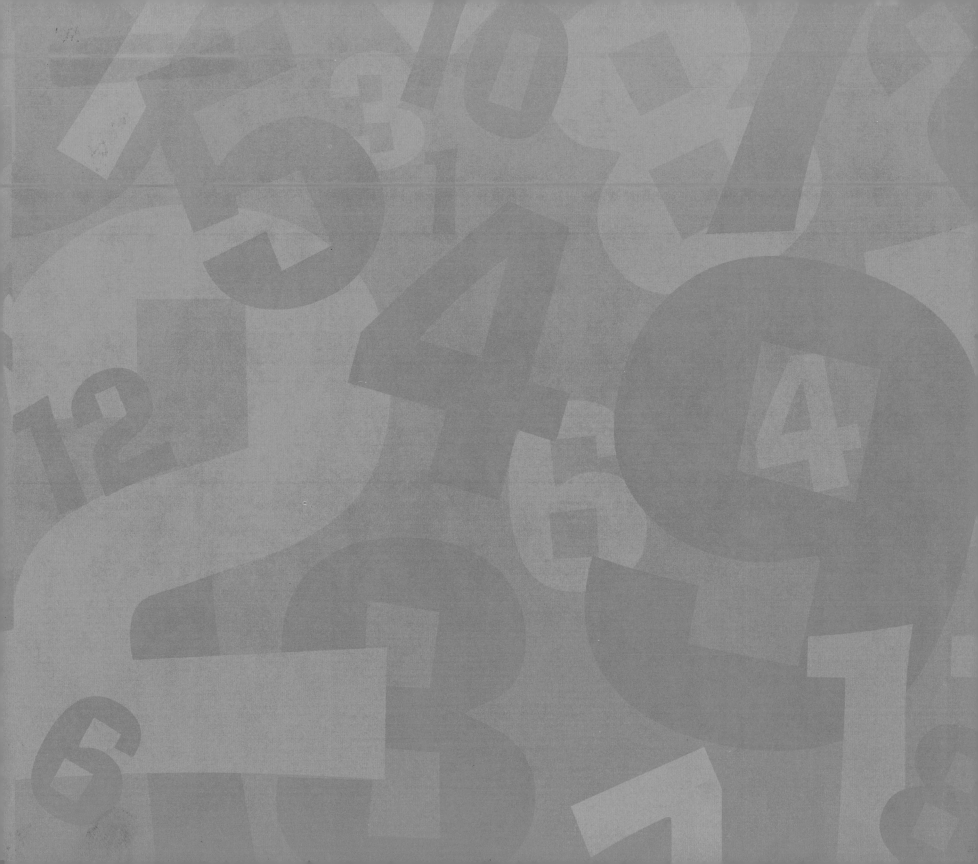

ONE big plan for making a big building.

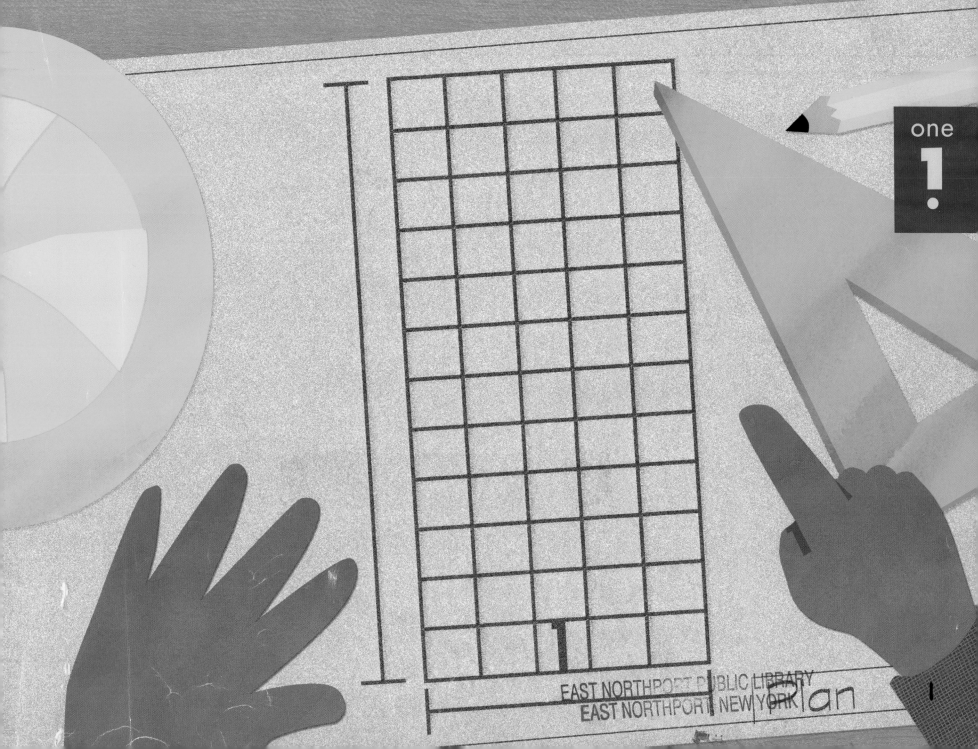

one
1!

TWO shovels dig a giant hole.

THREE dump trucks haul away the dirt.

three
3
...

3

FOUR pile drivers pound steel
into the ground.

4

FIVE concrete mixers rumble and roll.

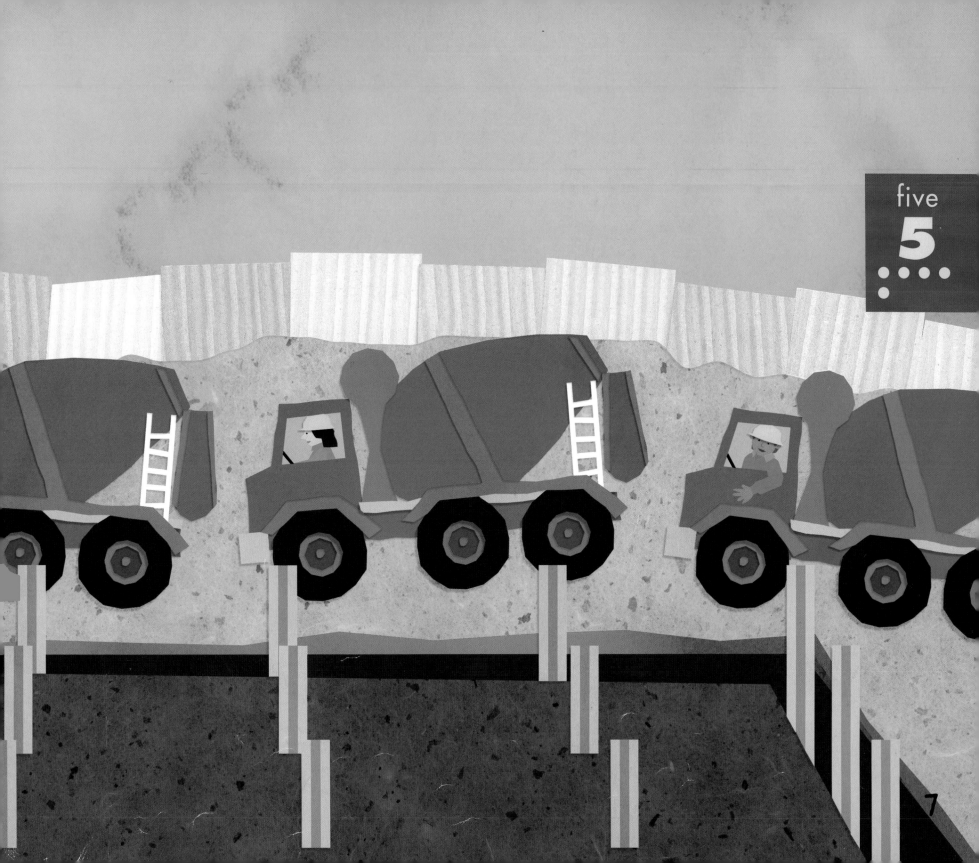

five
5
• • • • •

6

SIX metal beams
are lifted
by a crane.

SEVEN workers sit in the shade and take a break.

EIGHT bosses worry that the weather will turn bad.

12

EIGHT bosses worry that the weather will turn bad.

12

NINE wheelbarrows carry supplies.

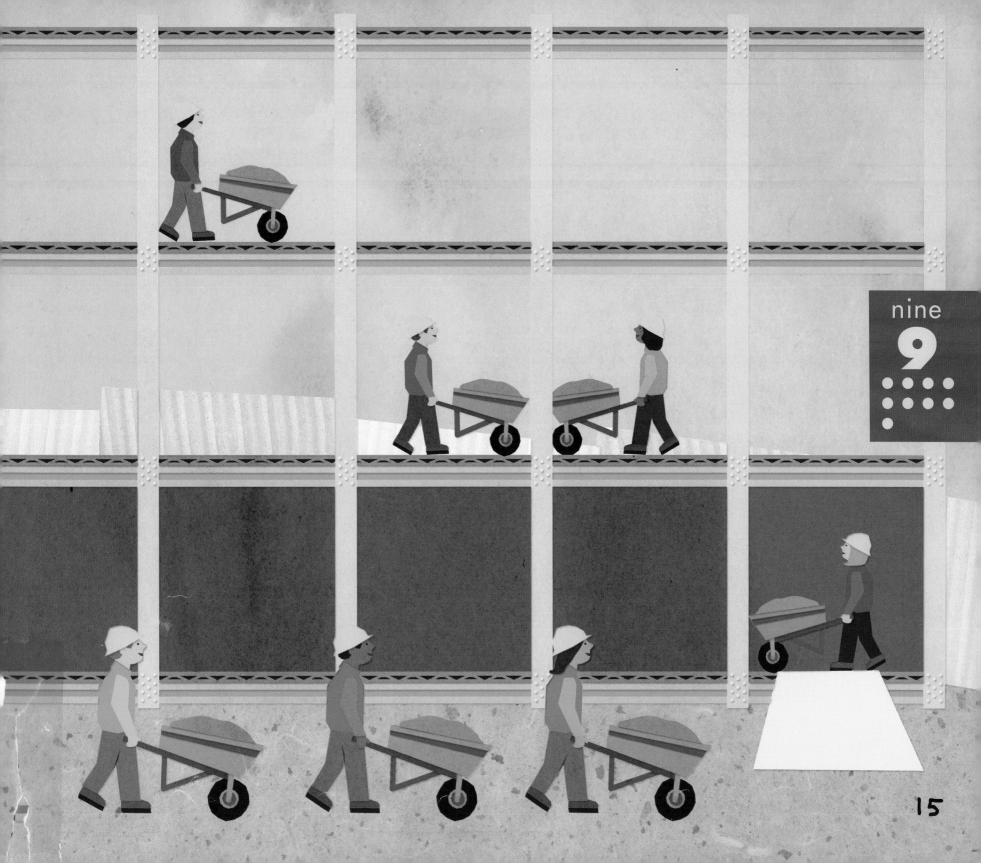

nine
9

15

TEN windows reflect the sky.

ten
10

17

ELEVEN painters finish the rooms and hallways.

eleven
11

19

twelve **12**

TWELVE stories tall,
the new building
gleams in the sun.

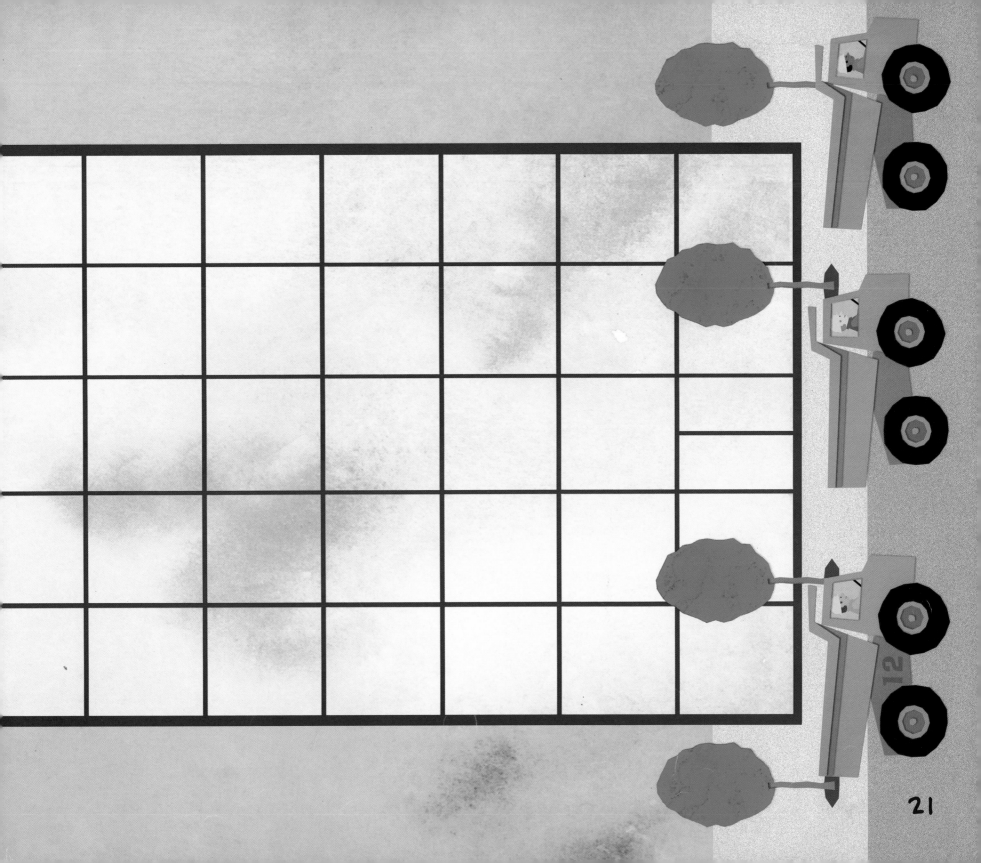

21

Fun Facts

 Before anything can be built, the soil needs to be cleared away for the building's foundation. The foundation supports the whole building!

 Almost every building has two main parts. The substructure, or foundation, is the part below the ground. The superstructure is the part above the ground.

 The world's tallest free-standing structure is the CN Tower in Toronto, Ontario. This tower is 1,815 feet (533 meters) tall!

 The beams of a building are like the bones of your body. Your bones help hold you up. Beams help hold up a building.

 Many people are needed to make a building complete. They include carpenters, electricians, plumbers, painters, and many others.

 Bad weather can make it unsafe for crews to work on a building. If crews have to stop working because of the weather, the building may take longer to finish.

 Architects are people who design buildings. Architects design houses, schools, sports stadiums, and movie theaters—just about any building you can imagine!

Find the Numbers

Now you have finished reading the story, but a surprise still awaits you.
Hidden in each picture is one of the numbers from 1 to 12. Can you find them all?

Key

1—middle window on bottom floor of plan

2—ready to be scooped up by right shovel

3—in the front wheel on the farthest right truck

4—just below the reel for the cable on the pile driver that is farthest left

5—on the boot of the worker emptying his cement truck

6—at the top of the crane's cable

7—the handle of the blue and black drink container

8—the top of the clipboard the woman is holding on page 12

9—in the pulley on page 14

10—on the front of the cart on page 16

11—on the bottom of the ladder on page 19

12—between the wheels on the body of the truck that is farthest left

Go on an Observation Walk

Counting is fun! Step outside your door, and practice counting by going on an observation walk in your neighborhood—or even your own yard. Ask an adult to go with you. On an observation walk, you notice the things all around you. Count the number of trees in your yard or on your block. Count the number of dogs you see. Count the number of windows on one side of your home. You can count everything!

Glossary

beam–a long, strong piece of metal, wood, or concrete that holds a building up

concrete–a substance made from sand and gravel, water, and cement. Cement is a gray powder made from limestone that becomes hard when it is mixed with water.

plan–a drawing that shows how to put a building together

story–a level of a building

On the Web

Fact Hound

Fact Hound offers a safe, fun way to find Web sites related to this book. All of the sites on Fact Hound have been researched by our staff.
http://www.facthound.com

1. Visit the Fact Hound home page.
2. Enter a search word related to this book, or type in this special code:140480580X.
3. Click on the FETCH IT button.

Your trusty Fact Hound will fetch the best sites for you!

Index

Acknowledgments

Thanks to our advisers for their expertise, research, and advice:

Stuart Farm, M.A.
Mathematics Lecturer,
University of North Dakota
Grand Forks, North Dakota

Susan Kesselring, M.A.
Literacy Educator
Rosemount-Apple Valley-Eagan
(Minnesota) School District

The editor would like to thank Donald E. Wolf, P.E., for his expert advice in preparing this book.

Managing Editor: Bob Temple
Creative Director: Terri Foley
Editor: Brenda Haugen
Editorial Adviser: Andrea Cascardi
Copy Editor: Sue Gregson
Designer: Nathan Gassman

Page production: Picture Window Books
The illustrations in this book were rendered digitally.

Picture Window Books
5115 Excelsior Boulevard
Suite 232
Minneapolis, MN 55416
1-877-845-8392
www.picturewindowbooks.com

Library of Congress Cataloging-in-Publication Data
Dahl, Michael.
One big building : a counting book about construction / written by Michael Dahl ; illustrated by Todd Ouren.
p. cm. — (Know your numbers)
Summary: A counting book that follows the construction of a building, from one plan to twelve stories. Readers are invited to find hidden numbers on an illustrated activity page. Includes bibliographical references and index.
ISBN 1-4048-0580-X (Reinforced Library Binding)
1. Building—Juvenile literature. 2. Counting—Juvenile literature.
[1. Building. 2. Counting. 3. Picture puzzles.] I. Ouren, Todd, ill. II. Title.
TH149 .D34 2004 513.2'11—dc22 [E]
2003020935